SEEKING TRUTH

QUESTIONS AND ANSWERS FROM THE WORD
OF GOD

JOHN J. KNOERNSCHILD

Edited by
JULIE PERSHING

GALLIVANT
PRESS

To God be the Glory

"I choose to believe the Bible because it is a reliable source of historical documents written by eyewitnesses during the lifetime of other eyewitnesses. They report supernatural events that took place in fulfillment of specific prophecies and claim that their writings are divine rather than human in origin."
  –Voddie Bauchman

CONTENTS

INTRODUCTION

During my spiritual journey, I've had deep conversations with God, asking various questions that weigh on my heart. Today, I want to share some of those questions and the personal insights I received in return. It is my hope and prayer that these revelations bring value to your life and touch your soul in a meaningful way.

I have been asked whether I believe every single word in the Bible is true. The Bible claims its own truthfulness, but I must acknowledge that not everything in the Bible is directly applicable to my life today or in the environment in which I live, especially if I do not use or understand it. For example, the Levitical laws from the past may not directly apply to my circumstances. However, this does not mean that it is wise for me to disregard all the wisdom and richness that the books of the Bible have to offer. It is important to carefully discern and apply the principles and teachings that are relevant to our lives.

When it comes to studying the Scriptures, I have been taught that there are certain rules to follow. However, it is important to note that the Bible itself wasn't written according to these rules. Some Bible teachers emphasize never taking a verse out of context, and I agree that it is beneficial to read and understand the entire context. It is also helpful to consider the writer's intended meaning within their historical and cultural context. Additionally, exploring different versions of the Bible can provide fresh perspectives.

A new approach I have learned is to read the Scripture and reflect on how those words personally speak to me in my own language. This means not relying solely on what Bible expositors have taught, but rather allowing the Holy Spirit to guide my understanding. I believe it is essential to seek enlightenment from the Holy Spirit, asking for the eyes of our hearts to be opened so that we can perceive the spiritual truths within the Scriptures.

It is beautifully expressed in Ephesians 1:17-19 (ESV):

"God of our Lord Jesus the Anointed, Father of Glory: I call out to You on behalf of Your people. Give them minds ready to receive wisdom and revelation so they will truly know You. Open the eyes of their hearts, and the hope You are calling them to embrace. Reveal to them the glorious riches You are preparing as their inheritance. Let them see the full extent of Your power that is at work in those of us who believe, and may it be done according to Your might and power."

I believe this passage encourages a spiritual understanding of the Scriptures.

I want to express my gratitude for your interest and willingness to engage in this conversation. May the Lord bless and keep you, and may His face shine upon you.

I sincerely pray this exchange is a blessing to you.

HOW TO USE THIS BOOK

This book is a collection of questions that have been on my mind and questions that people have asked me, all with the desire to find answers within the Word of God.

I've gathered these questions, explored them, and sought out scripture that can shed light on them. The goal is to provide accessible and insightful responses to a wide range of topics that we encounter in life.

Instead of presenting the questions randomly, the questions are organized into sections based on different themes. This way, you can easily navigate through the book and find answers that resonate with your own queries. Each section tackles specific areas of life and addresses the concerns and curiosities we often have.

In addition to the scriptures listed, there are pages for notes or to write relevant scriptures. My hope is that these connections will help you relate to the material and apply the lessons to your own experiences.

I genuinely hope that this book becomes a valuable resource for anyone seeking answers grounded in biblical principles. Whether you're simply curious, a devoted believer, or someone grappling with life's uncertainties, my aim is for the wisdom shared within these pages to bring you clarity, guidance, and comfort.

Thank you for joining me on this journey of exploration and discovery. Together, let's unlock the timeless truths of the Bible and discover answers to the questions that have touched our hearts and intrigued our minds.

ONE
LIFE QUESTIONS TO GOD

Daily Meditation:

Quiet yourself and mediate on the Word of God and listen to what he reveals to you.

What's my priority today?
What about my thoughts?
How did you arrive at that conclusion?
What's the reliability of my source?
What's the purpose of existence?
How do I glorify God?
Who am I?
Why am I here?
Where am I going?

TWO

THE WORD OF GOD

Question:

WHAT LASTS FOREVER?

What does the WORD say:

But the word of the Lord remains forever. And this word is the good news that was preached to you.

1 PETER 1:25 ESV

Heaven and earth will pass away, but my words will not pass away.

MATTHEW 24:35 ESV

The grass withers, the flower fades, but the word of our God will stand forever.

ISAIAH 40:8 ESV

But the day of the Lord will come like a thief, and then the heavens will pass away with a roar, and the heavenly bodies will be burned up and dissolved, and the earth and the works that are done on it will be exposed.

2 PETER 3:10 ESV

And I am sure of this, that he who began a good work in you will bring it to completion at the day of Jesus Christ.

PHILIPPIANS 1:6 ESV

Who will sustain you to the end, guiltless in the day of our Lord Jesus Christ.

1 CORINTHIANS 1:8 ESV

But because of your hard and impenitent heart you are storing up wrath for yourself on the day of wrath when God's righteous judgment will be revealed.

ROMANS 2:5 ESV

Question:

WHY IS THE WORD OF GOD IMPORTANT?

What does the WORD say:

But he answered, "It is written, "'Man shall not live by bread alone, but by every word that comes from the mouth of God.'"

MATTHEW 4:4 ESV

Question:

WHAT ENDURES FOREVER?

What does the WORD say:

Give thanks to the Lord, for he is good, for his steadfast love endures forever. Give thanks to the God of gods, for his steadfast love endures forever. Give thanks to the Lord of lords, for his steadfast love endures forever; to him who alone does great wonders, for his steadfast love endures forever; to him who by understanding made the heavens, for his steadfast love endures forever

PSALM 136:1-26 ESV

Since you have been born again, not of perishable seed but of imperishable, through the living and abiding word of God; for "All flesh is like grass and all its glory like the flower of grass. The grass withers, and the flower falls, but the word of the Lord remains forever." And this word is the good news that was preached to you.

1 PETER 1:23-25 ESV

Question:

WHAT SHOULD I LIVE BY?

What does the WORD say:

But he answered, It is written, Man shall not live by bread alone, but by every word that comes from the mouth of God.

MATTHEW 4:4 ESV

Question:

HOW DO WE HAVE THE RIGHT TO BE
CHILDREN OF GOD?

What does the WORD say:

But to all who did receive him, who believed in his name, he gave
the right to become children of God

JOHN 1:12 ESV

Question:

WHAT'S EXALTED ABOVE ALL THINGS?

What does the WORD say:

I bow down toward your holy temple and give thanks to your name for your steadfast love and your faithfulness, for you have exalted above all things your name and your word.

PSALM 138:2 ESV

All Scripture is breathed out by God and profitable for teaching, for reproof, for correction, and for training in righteousness

2 TIMOTHY 3:16 ESV

Now the Lord is the Spirit, and where the Spirit of the Lord is, there is freedom.

2 CORINTHIANS 3:17 ESV

When Jesus had spoken these words, he lifted up his eyes to heaven, and said, "Father, the hour has come; glorify your Son that the Son may glorify you, since you have given him authority over all flesh, to give eternal life to all whom you have given him. And this is eternal life, that they know you the only true God, and Jesus Christ whom you have sent. I glorified you on earth, having accomplished the work that you gave me to do. And now, Father, glorify me in your own presence with the glory that I had with you before the world existed.

JOHN 17:1-26 ESV

Question:

WHAT IS GOD'S WILL ACCORDING TO THE
WORD?

What does the WORD say:

God's ultimate will is the advancement of his kingdom:

In the time of those kings, the God of heaven will set up a kingdom
that will never be destroyed, nor will it be left to another people. It
will crush all those kingdoms and bring them to an end, but it will
itself endure forever.

DANIEL 2:44 NIV

His glorification:

So whether you eat or drink or whatever you do, do it all for the
glory of God.

1 CORINTHIANS 10:31 NIV

*And the salvation and sanctification of his children through his
son, Jesus Christ:*

The Lord is not slow in keeping his promise, as some understand
slowness. Instead he is patient with you, not wanting anyone to
perish, but everyone to come to repentance.

2 PETER 3:9 NIV

It is his desire to be in a loving relationship with us first, and for us to practice good deeds secondly:

> For this reason, since the day we heard about you, we have not stopped praying for you. We continually ask God to fill you with the knowledge of his will through all the wisdom and understanding that the Spirit gives, so that you may live a life worthy of the Lord and please him in every way: bearing fruit in every good work, growing in the knowledge of God, being strengthened with all power according to his glorious might so that you may have great endurance and patience, and giving joyful thanks to the Father, who has qualified you to share in the inheritance of his holy people in the kingdom of light. For he has rescued us from the dominion of darkness and brought us into the kingdom of the Son he loves, in whom we have redemption, the forgiveness of sins.

COLOSSIANS 1:9-14 NIV

> For we are God's handiwork, created in Christ Jesus to do good works, which God prepared in advance for us to do.

EPHESIANS 2:10

Question:

DOES GOD CARE ABOUT THE DETAILS IN
THE LAW?

What does the WORD say:

For truly, I say to you, until heaven and earth pass away, not an iota, not a dot, will pass from the Law until all is accomplished.

MATTHEW 5:18 ESV

THREE
THE WILL OF GOD

Question:

What is your will?

What does the WORD say:

I can do nothing on my own. As I hear, I judge, and my judgment is just, because I seek not my own will but the will of him who sent me.

JOHN 5:30 ESV

Do not be conformed to this world, but be transformed by the renewal of your mind, that by testing you may discern what is the will of God, what is good and acceptable and perfect.

ROMANS 12:2 ESV

Give thanks in all circumstances; for this is the will of God in Christ Jesus for you.

1 THESSALONIANS 5:18 ESV

For this is the will of God, that by doing good you should put to silence the ignorance of foolish people.

1 PETER 2:15 ESV

For this is the will of God, your sanctification: that you abstain from sexual immorality.

1 THESSALONIANS 4:3

Your kingdom come, your will be done, on earth as it is in heaven.

MATTHEW 6:10 ESV

If anyone's will is to do God's will, he will know whether the teaching is from God or whether I am speaking on my own authority.

JOHN 7:17 ESV

The Lord is not slow to fulfill his promise as some count slowness, but is patient toward you, not wishing that any should perish, but that all should reach repentance.

2 PETER 3:9 ESV

Therefore do not be foolish, but understand what the will of the Lord is.

EPHESIANS 5:17 ESV

Therefore do not throw away your confidence, which has a great reward. For you have need of endurance, so that when you have done the will of God you may receive what is promised.

HEBREWS 10:35-36 ESV

For I know the plans I have for you, declares the Lord, plans for welfare and not for evil, to give you a future and a hope. Then you will call upon me and come and pray to me, and I will hear you. You will seek me and find me, when you seek me with all your heart. I will be found by you, declares the Lord, and I will restore your fortunes and gather you from all the nations and all the places where I have driven you, declares the Lord, and I will bring you back to the place from which I sent you into exile.

JEREMIAH 29:11-14 ESV

Your word is a lamp to my feet and a light to my path.

PSALM 119:105 ESV

Who desires all people to be saved and to come to the knowledge of the truth.

1 TIMOTHY 2:4 ESV

Trust in the Lord with all your heart, and do not lean on your own understanding. In all your ways acknowledge him, and he will make straight your paths.

PROVERBS 3:5-6 ESV

Not until halfway through the festival did Jesus go up to the temple courts and begin to teach. The Jews there were amazed and asked, "How did this man get such learning without having been taught?"

Jesus answered, "My teaching is not my own. It comes from the one who sent me. Anyone who chooses to do the will of God will find out whether my teaching comes from God or whether I speak on my own. Whoever speaks on their own does so to gain personal glory, but he who seeks the glory of the one who sent him is a man of truth; there is nothing false about him.

JOHN 7:14-18 NIV

Now may the God of peace who brought again from the dead our Lord Jesus, the great shepherd of the sheep, by the blood of the eternal covenant, equip you with everything good that you may do his will, working in us that which is pleasing in his sight, through Jesus Christ, to whom be glory forever and ever. Amen.

HEBREWS 13:20-21 ESV

For God so loved the world, that he gave his only Son, that whoever believes in him should not perish but have eternal life.

JOHN 3:16 ESV

If we confess our sins, he is faithful and just to forgive us our sins and to cleanse us from all unrighteousness.

1 JOHN 1:9 ESV

I can do all things through him who strengthens me.

PHILIPPIANS 4:13 ESV

Jesus says, "Not everyone who says to me, 'Lord, Lord,' will enter the kingdom of heaven, but only the one who does the will of my Father who is in heaven."

MATTHEW 7:21

Fear not, for I am with you; be not dismayed, for I am your God; I will strengthen you, I will help you, I will uphold you with my righteous right hand.

ISAIAH 41:10 ESV

But seek first the kingdom of God and his righteousness, and all these things will be added to you.

MATTHEW 6:33 ESV

For the word of God is living and active, sharper than any two-edged sword, piercing to the division of soul and of spirit, of joints and of marrow, and discerning the thoughts and intentions of the heart.

HEBREWS 4:12 ESV

And the world is passing away along with its desires, but whoever does the will of God abides forever.

1 JOHN 2:17 ESV

For all that is in the world—the desires of the flesh and the desires of the eyes and pride in possessions—is not from the Father but is from the world. And the world is passing away along with its desires, but whoever does the will of God abides forever.

1 JOHN 2:16-17 ESV

For it is better to suffer for doing good, if that should be God's will, than for doing evil.

1 PETER 3:17 ESV

And we know that for those who love God all things work together for good, for those who are called according to his purpose.

ROMANS 8:28 ESV

Seek the Lord and his strength; seek his presence continually!

1 CHRONICLES 16:11 ESV

For the wages of sin is death, but the free gift of God is eternal life in Christ Jesus our Lord.

ROMANS 6:23 ESV

For whoever does the will of God, he is my brother and sister and mother.

MARK 3:35 ESV

Therefore let those who suffer according to God's will entrust their souls to a faithful Creator while doing good.

1 PETER 4:19 ESV

If any of you lacks wisdom, let him ask God, who gives generously to all without reproach, and it will be given him.

JAMES 1:5 ESV

No temptation has overtaken you that is not common to man. God is faithful, and he will not let you be tempted beyond your ability, but with the temptation he will also provide the way of escape, that you may be able to endure it.

1 CORINTHIANS 10:13 ESV

Instead you ought to say, "If the Lord wills, we will live and do this or that."

JAMES 4:15 ESV

The Lord your God is in your midst, a mighty one who will save; he will rejoice over you with gladness; he will quiet you by his love; he will exult over you with loud singing.

ZEPHANIAH 3:17 ESV

For I have come down from heaven, not to do my own will but the will of him who sent me. And this is the will of him who sent me, that I should lose nothing of all that he has given me, but raise it up on the last day. For this is the will of my Father, that everyone who looks on the Son and believes in him should have eternal life, and I will raise him up on the last day.

JOHN 6:38-40 ESV

And my God will supply every need of yours according to his riches in glory in Christ Jesus.

PHILIPPIANS 4:19 ESV

I appeal to you therefore, brothers, by the mercies of God, to present your bodies as a living sacrifice, holy and acceptable to God, which is your spiritual worship. Do not be conformed to this world, but be transformed by the renewal of your mind, that by testing you may discern what is the will of God, what is good and acceptable and perfect.

ROMANS 12:1-2 ESV

For I know the plans I have for you, declares the Lord, plans for welfare and not for evil, to give you a future and a hope. Then you will call upon me and come and pray to me, and I will hear you. You will seek me and find me, when you seek me with all your heart.

JEREMIAH 29:11-13 ESV

Many are the plans in the mind of a man, but it is the purpose of the Lord that will stand.

PROVERBS 19:21 ESV

Pray then like this: Our Father in heaven, hallowed be your name. Your kingdom come, your will be done, on earth as it is in heaven. Give us this day our daily bread, and forgive us our debts, as we also have forgiven our debtors. And lead us not into temptation, but deliver us from evil.

MATTHEW 6:9-13 ESV

The Lord is my shepherd; I shall not want. He makes me lie down in green pastures. He leads me beside still waters. He restores my soul. He leads me in paths of righteousness for his name's sake. Even though I walk through the valley of the shadow of death, I will fear no evil, for you are with me; your rod and your staff, they comfort me. You prepare a table before me in the presence of my enemies; you anoint my head with oil; my cup overflows.

PSALM 23:1-6 ESV

For God gave us a spirit not of fear but of power and love and self-control.

2 TIMOTHY 1:7 ESV

Have I not commanded you? Be strong and courageous. Do not be frightened, and do not be dismayed, for the Lord your God is with you wherever you go.

JOSHUA 1:9 ESV

For this is the will of my Father, that everyone who looks on the Son and believes in him should have eternal life, and I will raise him up on the last day.

JOHN 6:40 ESV

Not everyone who says to me, 'Lord, Lord,' will enter the kingdom of heaven, but the one who does the will of my Father who is in heaven. On that day many will say to me, 'Lord, Lord, did we not prophesy in your name, and cast out demons in your name, and do many mighty works in your name?' And then will I declare to them, 'I never knew you; depart from me, you workers of lawlessness.'

MATTHEW 7:21-23 ESV

And he who searches hearts knows what is the mind of the Spirit, because the Spirit intercedes for the saints according to the will of God.

ROMANS 8:27 ESV

Finally, then, brothers, we ask and urge you in the Lord Jesus, that as you received from us how you ought to walk and to please God, just as you are doing, that you do so more and more. For you know what instructions we gave you through the Lord Jesus. For this is the will of God, your sanctification: that you abstain from sexual immorality; that each one of you know how to control his own body in holiness and honor, not in the passion of lust like the Gentiles who do not know God; that no one transgress and wrong his brother in this matter, because the Lord is an avenger in all these things, as we told you beforehand and solemnly warned you. For God has not called us for impurity, but in holiness. Therefore whoever disregards this, disregards not man but God, who gives his Holy Spirit to you.

1 THESSALONIANS 4:1-8

For this reason, since the day we heard about you, we have not stopped praying for you. We continually ask God to fill you with the knowledge of his will through all the wisdom and under-standing that the Spirit gives, so that you may live a life worthy of the Lord and please him in every way: bearing fruit in every good work, growing in the knowledge of God, being strengthened with all power according to his glorious might so that you may have great endurance and patience, 12 and giving joyful thanks to the Father, who has qualified you to share in the inheritance of his holy people in the kingdom of light. For he has rescued us from the dominion of darkness and brought us into the kingdom of the Son he loves, in whom we have redemption, the forgiveness of sins.

COLOSSIANS 1:9-14

But God shows his love for us in that while we were still sinners, Christ died for us.

ROMANS 5:8 ESV

For this is the will of God, your sanctification: that you abstain from sexual immorality; that each one of you know how to control his own body in holiness and honor, not in the passion of lust like the Gentiles who do not know God.

1 THESSALONIANS 4:3-5 ESV

In the beginning was the Word, and the Word was with God, and the Word was God.

JOHN 1:1 ESV

We know that God does not listen to sinners, but if anyone is a worshiper of God and does his will, God listens to him.

JOHN 9:31 ESV

I have said these things to you, that in me you may have peace. In the world you will have tribulation. But take heart; I have overcome the world.

JOHN 16:33 ESV

Teach me to do your will, for you are my God! Let your good Spirit lead me on level ground!

PSALM 143:10 ESV

And without faith it is impossible to please him, for whoever would draw near to God must believe that he exists and that he rewards those who seek him.

HEBREWS 11:6 ESV

Look carefully then how you walk, not as unwise but as wise, making the best use of the time, because the days are evil. Therefore do not be foolish, but understand what the will of the Lord is. And do not get drunk with wine, for that is debauchery, but be filled with the Spirit, addressing one another in psalms and hymns and spiritual songs, singing and making melody to the Lord with your heart.

EPHESIANS 5:15-19 ESV

Ah, land of whirring wings that is beyond the rivers of Cush, which sends ambassadors by the sea, in vessels of papyrus on the waters! Go, you swift messengers, to a nation, tall and smooth, to a people feared near and far, a nation mighty and conquering, whose land the rivers divide. All you inhabitants of the world, you who dwell on the earth, when a signal is raised on the mountains, look! When a trumpet is blown, hear! For thus the Lord said to me: "I will quietly look from my dwelling like clear heat in sunshine, like a cloud of dew in the heat of harvest." For before the harvest, when the blossom is over, and the flower becomes a ripening grape, he cuts off the shoots with pruning hooks, and the spreading branches he lops off and clears away. ...

ISAIAH 18:1-7 ESV

And he said to all, "If anyone would come after me, let him deny himself and take up his cross daily and follow me.

LUKE 9:23 ESV

The grass withers, the flower fades, but the word of our God will stand forever.

ISAIAH 40:8 ESV

I appeal to you therefore, brothers, by the mercies of God, to present your bodies as a living sacrifice, holy and acceptable to God, which is your spiritual worship. Do not be conformed to this world, but be transformed by the renewal of your mind, that by testing you may discern what is the will of God, what is good and acceptable and perfect.

ROMANS 12:1-2 ESV

Question:

DO YOU DELIGHT TO DO HIS WILL?

What does the WORD say:

I delight to do your will, O my God; your law is within my heart.

PSALM 40:8 ESV

Every word of God proves true; he is a shield to those who take refuge in him.

PROVERBS 30:5 ESV

I have said these things to you, that in me you may have peace. In the world you will have tribulation. But take heart; I have overcome the world.

JOHN 16:33 ESV

Behold, in this you are not right. I will answer you, for God is greater than man. Why do you contend against him, saying, 'He will answer none of man's words'? For God speaks in one way, and in two, though man does not perceive it. In a dream, in a vision of the night, when deep sleep falls on men, while they slumber on their beds, then he opens the ears of men and terrifies them with warnings.

JOB 33:12-16 ESV

For it is God who works in you, both to will and to work for his good pleasure.

PHILIPPIANS 2:13 ESV

Finally, be strong in the Lord and in the strength of his might. Put on the whole armor of God, that you may be able to stand against the schemes of the devil. For we do not wrestle against flesh and blood, but against the rulers, against the authorities, against the cosmic powers over this present darkness, against the spiritual forces of evil in the heavenly places. Therefore take up the whole armor of God, that you may be able to withstand in the evil day, and having done all, to stand firm. Stand therefore, having fastened on the belt of truth, and having put on the breastplate of right-eousness, and, as shoes for your feet, having put on the readiness given by the gospel of peace. In all circumstances take up the shield of faith, with which you can extinguish all the flaming darts of the evil one; and take the helmet of salvation, and the sword of the Spirit, which is the word of God.

EPHESIANS 6:10-17 ESV

O Lord, our Lord, how majestic is your name in all the earth! You have set your glory above the heavens. Out of the mouth of babies and infants, you have established strength because of your foes, to still the enemy and the avenger. When I look at your heavens, the work of your fingers, the moon and the stars, which you have set in place, what is man that you are mindful of him, and the son of man that you care for him? Yet you have made him a little lower than the heavenly beings and crowned him with glory and honor. You have given him dominion over the works of your hands; you have put all things under his feet, all sheep and oxen, and also the beasts of the field, the birds of the heavens, and the fish of the sea, what-ever passes along the paths of the seas. O LORD, our Lord, how majestic is your name in all the earth!

PSALM 8:1-9 ESV

For I will satisfy the weary soul, and every languishing soul I will replenish.

JEREMIAH 31:25 ESV

And now, behold, the Lord has kept me alive, just as he said, these forty-five years since the time that the Lord spoke this word to Moses, while Israel walked in the wilderness. And now, behold, I am this day eighty-five years old. I am still as strong today as I was in the day that Moses sent me; my strength now is as my strength was then, for war and for going and coming.

JOSHUA 14:10-11 ESV

For it is God who works in you, both to will and to work for his good pleasure. Do all things without grumbling or questioning, that you may be blameless and innocent, children of God without blemish in the midst of a crooked and twisted generation, among whom you shine as lights in the world, holding fast to the word of life, so that in the day of Christ I may be proud that I did not run in vain or labor in vain. Even if I am to be poured out as a drink offering upon the sacrificial offering of your faith, I am glad and rejoice with you all.

PHILIPPIANS 2:13-23 ESV

And what is the immeasurable greatness of his power toward us who believe, according to the working of his great might that he worked in Christ when he raised him from the dead and seated him at his right hand in the heavenly places

EPHESIANS 1:19-20 ESV

Do not be slothful in zeal, be fervent in spirit, serve the Lord.

ROMANS 12:11 ESV

But seek first the kingdom of God and his righteousness, and all these things will be added to you.

MATTHEW 6:33 ESV

The thief comes only to steal and kill and destroy. I came that they may have life and have it abundantly.

JOHN 10:10 ESV

But Martha was distracted with much serving. And she went up to him and said, "Lord, do you not care that my sister has left me to serve alone? Tell her then to help me." But the Lord answered her, "Martha, Martha, you are anxious and troubled about many things, but one thing is necessary. Mary has chosen the good portion, which will not be taken away from her."

LUKE 10:40-42 ESV

In their case the god of this world has blinded the minds of the unbelievers, to keep them from seeing the light of the gospel of the glory of Christ, who is the image of God.

2 CORINTHIANS 4:4 ESV

Whoever believes in him is not condemned, but whoever does not believe is condemned already, because he has not believed in the name of the only Son of God. And this is the judgment: the light has come into the world, and people loved the darkness rather than the light because their works were evil. For everyone who does wicked things hates the light and does not come to the light, lest his works should be exposed.

JOHN 3:18-20 ESV

In the same way, let your light shine before others, so that they may see your good works and give glory to your Father who is in heaven.

MATTHEW 5:16 ESV

Then he said to them, "Go your way. Eat the fat and drink sweet wine and send portions to anyone who has nothing ready, for this day is holy to our Lord. And do not be grieved, for the joy of the Lord is your strength."

NEHEMIAH 8:10 ESV

I know how to be brought low, and I know how to abound. In any and every circumstance, I have learned the secret of facing plenty and hunger, abundance and need. I can do all things through him who strengthens me.

PHILIPPIANS 4:12-13 ESV

If the iron is blunt, and one does not sharpen the edge, he must use more strength, but wisdom helps one to succeed.

ECCLESIASTES 10:10

Question:

WHERE DOES MY HELP COME FROM?

What does the WORD say:

I lift up my eyes to the hills. From where does my help come? My help comes from the Lord, who made heaven and earth.

PSALM 121:1-2 ESV

Summon your power, O God, the power, O God, by which you have worked for us.

PSALM 68:28 ESV

For in him we live and move and have our being; as even some of your own poets have said, For we are indeed his offspring.

ACTS 17:28 ESV

Why do you spend your money for that which is not bread, and your labor for that which does not satisfy? Listen diligently to me, and eat what is good, and delight yourselves in rich food.

ISAIAH 55:2 ESV

For God so loved the world, that he gave his only Son, that whoever believes in him should not perish but have eternal life. For God did not send his Son into the world to condemn the world, but in order that the world might be saved through him.

JOHN 3:16-17 ESV

FOUR
BLESSINGS

Question:

WHO IS BLESSED?

What does the WORD say:

Blessed are those whose way is blameless, who walk in the law of the Lord! Blessed are those who keep his testimonies, who seek him with their whole heart, who also do no wrong, but walk in his ways! You have commanded your precepts to be kept diligently. Oh that my ways may be steadfast in keeping your statutes!

PSALM 119:1-176 ESV

Blessed is the man who trusts in the Lord, whose trust is the Lord. He is like a tree planted by water, that sends out its roots by the stream, and does not fear when heat comes, for its leaves remain green, and is not anxious in the year of drought, for it does not cease to bear fruit.

JEREMIAH 17:7-8 ESV

Question:

WHAT SHOULD I TREASURE AND COLLECT?

What does the WORD say:

Do not lay up for yourselves treasures on earth, where moth and rust destroy and where thieves break in and steal, but lay up for yourselves treasures in heaven, where neither moth nor rust destroys and where thieves do not break in and steal. For where your treasure is, there your heart will be also.

MATTHEW 6:19-21 ESV

Question:

WHAT MUST I DO TO HEAR THE WORDS, "WELL DONE, GOOD AND FAITHFUL SERVANT, ENTER INTO MY JOY."

What does the WORD say:

Simon Peter, a servant and apostle of Jesus Christ, To those who through the righteousness of our God and Savior Jesus Christ have received a faith as precious as ours: Grace and peace be yours in abundance through the knowledge of God and of Jesus our Lord. His divine power e of him who called us by his own glory and goodness. Through these he has given us his very great and precious promises, so that through them you may participate in the divine nature, having escaped the corruption in the world caused by evil desires.

For this very reason, make every effort to add to your faith goodness; and to goodness, knowledge; and to knowledge, self-control; and to self-control, perseverance; and to perseverance, godliness; and to godliness, mutual affection; and to mutual affection, love. For if you possess these qualities in increasing measure, they will keep you from being ineffective and unproductive in your knowledge of our Lord Jesus Christ. But whoever does not have them is nearsighted and blind, forgetting that they have been cleansed from their past sins.

Therefore, my brothers and sisters, make every effort to confirm your calling and election. For if you do these things, you will never stumble, and you will receive a rich welcome into the eternal kingdom of our Lord and Savior Jesus Christ.

2 PETER 1:1-11 NIV

FIVE

CREATION

Question:

HOW DID DARK AND LIGHT COME ABOUT?

What does the WORD say:

In the beginning, God created the heavens and the earth. The earth was without form and void, and darkness was over the face of the deep. And the Spirit of God was hovering over the face of the waters. And God said, "Let there be light," and there was light. And God saw that the light was good. And God separated the light from the darkness. God called the light Day, and the darkness he called Night. And there was evening and there was morning, the first day.

GENESIS 1:1-31 ESV

This is the message we have heard from him and proclaim to you, that God is light, and in him is no darkness at all.

1 JOHN 1:5 ESV

Then the angel showed me the river of the water of life, bright as crystal, flowing from the throne of God and of the Lamb through the middle of the street of the city; also, on either side of the river, the tree of life with its twelve kinds of fruit, yielding its fruit each month. The leaves of the tree were for the healing of the nations. No longer will there be anything accursed, but the throne of God and of the Lamb will be in it, and his servants will worship him. They will see his face, and his name will be on their foreheads. And night will be no more. They will need no light of lamp or sun, for the Lord God will be their light, and they will reign forever and ever.

REVELATION 22:1-21 ESV

SIX

ETERNAL LIFE

Question:

HOW DO I GAIN ETERNAL LIFE?

What does the WORD say:

For the wages of sin is death, but the gift of God is eternal life in Christ Jesus our Lord.

ROMANS 6:23 NIV

I give them eternal life, and they shall never perish; no one will snatch them out of my hand.

JOHN 10:28 NIV

For God so loved the world that he gave his one and only Son, that whoever believes in him shall not perish but have eternal life.

JOHN 3:16

Question:

WHAT MUST I DO TO BE SAVED?

What does the WORD say:

Believe in the Lord Jesus, and you will be saved.

ACTS 16:31 NIV

Question:

WHAT IS THE ROMANS ROAD?

What does the WORD say:

There is no one righteous, not even one.

ROMANS 3:10 NIV

For all have sinned and fall short of the glory of God.

ROMANS 3:23 NIV

For the Wages of sin is death, but the gift of God is eternal life in Christ Jesus our Lord.

ROMANS 6:23 NIV

But God demonstrates his own love towards us in this: While we were still sinners, Christ died for us.

ROMANS 5:8 NIV

For everyone who calls on the name of the Lord will be saved.

ROMANS 10:13 NIV

Question:

WHERE DOES MY HELP COME FROM?

What does the WORD say:

A Song of Ascents. I lift up my eyes to the hills. From where does my help come? My help comes from the Lord, who made heaven and earth.

PSALM 121:1-2 ESV

Summon your power, O God, the power, O God, by which you have worked for us.

PSALM 68:28 ESV

For In him we live and move and have our being; as even some of your own poets have said, For we are indeed his offspring.

ACTS 17:28 ESV

Why do you spend your money for that which is not bread, and your labor for that which does not satisfy? Listen diligently to me, and eat what is good, and delight yourselves in rich food.

ISAIAH 55:2 ESV

For God so loved the world, that he gave his only Son, that whoever believes in him should not perish but have eternal life. For God did not send his Son into the world to condemn the world, but in order that the world might be saved through him.

JOHN 3:16-17 ESV

SEVEN
FAITH

Question:

WHAT PLEASES GOD?

What does the WORD say:

And without faith it is impossible to please God, because anyone
who comes to him must believe that he exists and that he rewards
those who earnestly seek him.

HEBREW 11:6 NIV

Question:

WHAT SHOULD WE WALK IN?

What does the WORD say:

For we are his workmanship, created in Christ Jesus for good works, which God prepared beforehand, that we should walk in them.

EPHESIANS 2:10 ESV

Lord, you have been our dwelling place in all generations. Before the mountains were brought forth, or ever you had formed the earth and the world, from everlasting to everlasting you are God. You return man to dust and say, "Return, O children of man!" For a thousand years in your sight are but as yesterday when it is past, or as a watch in the night. You sweep them away as with a flood; they are like a dream, like grass that is renewed in the morning

PSALM 90:1-6 ESV

Question:

WHAT'S EXALTED ABOVE ALL THINGS?

What does the WORD say:

I bow down toward your holy temple and give thanks to your name for your steadfast love and your faithfulness, for you have exalted above all things your name and your word.

PSALM 138:2 ESV

All Scripture is breathed out by God and profitable for teaching, for reproof, for correction, and for training in righteousness.

2 TIMOTHY 3:16 ESV

Now the Lord is the Spirit, and where the Spirit of the Lord is, there is freedom.

2 CORINTHIANS 3:17 ESV

When Jesus had spoken these words, he lifted up his eyes to heaven, and said, "Father, the hour has come; glorify your Son that the Son may glorify you, since you have given him authority over all flesh, to give eternal life to all whom you have given him. And this is eternal life, that they know you the only true God, and Jesus Christ whom you have sent. I glorified you on earth, having accomplished the work that you gave me to do. And now, Father, glorify me in your own presence with the glory that I had with you before the world existed.

JOHN 17:1-26 ESV

Question:

WHAT IS FAITH?

What does the WORD say:

Now faith is the assurance of things hoped for, the conviction of things not seen.

HEBREWS 11:1 ESV

Question:

WHERE DOES MY HELP COME FROM?

What does the WORD say:

I lift up my eyes to the hills. From where does my help come? My help comes from the Lord, who made heaven and earth.

PSALM 121:1-2 ESV

Summon your power, O God, the power, O God, by which you have worked for us.

PSALM 68:28 ESV

For in him we live and move and have our being; as even some of your own poets have said, For we are indeed his offspring.

ACTS 17:28 ESV

Why do you spend your money for that which is not bread, and your labor for that which does not satisfy? Listen diligently to me, and eat what is good, and delight yourselves in rich food.

ISAIAH 55:2 ESV

For God so loved the world, that he gave his only Son, that whoever believes in him should not perish but have eternal life. For God did not send his Son into the world to condemn the world, but in order that the world might be saved through him.

JOHN 3:16-17 ESV

EIGHT
FORGIVENESS

Question:

WHAT IS THE ASSURANCE OF FORGIVENESS?

What does the WORD say:

If we confess our sins, he is faithful and just to forgive us our sins and to cleanse us from all unrighteousness.

1 JOHN 1:9 ESV

But God demonstrates his own love for us in this: While we were still sinners, Christ died for us.

ROMANS 5:8 NIV

Everyone who calls upon the name of the Lord will be saved.

ROMANS 10:13 NIV

In action:

A simple prayer for you:

Dear Father, Forgive my sins, I believe and trust in you Jesus. I open my heart. Come in Jesus. By the power of the Holy Spirit. Thank you for eternal life. Guide me in the way I should go. Amen

NINE

HEAVEN

Question:

WHAT WILL HEAVEN BE LIKE?

What does the WORD say:

Then I saw a new heaven and a new earth, for the first heaven and
the first earth had passed away, and the sea was no more. And I saw
the holy city, new Jerusalem, coming down out of heaven from
God, prepared as a bride adorned for her husband. And I heard a
loud voice from the throne saying, "Behold, the dwelling place of
God is with man. He will dwell with them, and they will be his
people, and God himself will be with them as their God. He will
wipe away every tear from their eyes, and death shall be no more,
neither shall there be mourning, nor crying, nor pain anymore, for
the former things have passed away." And he who was seated on
the throne said, "Behold, I am making all things new." Also he said,
"Write this down, for these words are trustworthy and true."

REVELATION 21:1-27 ESV

Do you not know that you are God's temple and that God's Spirit dwells in you?

1 CORINTHIANS 3:16 ESV

Question:

WHAT SHOULD I TREASURE?

What does the WORD say:

Do not lay up for yourselves treasures on earth, where moth and rust destroy and where thieves break in and steal, but lay up for yourselves treasures in heaven, where neither moth nor rust destroys and where thieves do not break in and steal. For where your treasure is, there your heart will be also.

MATTHEW 6:19-21 ESV

TEN
JESUS

Question:

WHO IS THE WAY? WHAT WAY SHOULD I GO?

What does the WORD say:

Jesus said to him, "I am the way, and the truth, and the life. No one comes to the Father except through me.

JOHN 14:6 ESV

And so, from the day we heard, we have not ceased to pray for you, asking that you may be filled with the knowledge of his will in all spiritual wisdom and understanding.

COLOSSIANS 1:9 ESV

Saying, Father, if you are willing, remove this cup from me. Nevertheless, not my will, but yours, be done.

LUKE 22:42 ESV

And whatever you ask in prayer, you will receive, if you have faith.

MATTHEW 21:22 ESV

For God so loved the world, that he gave his only Son, that whoever believes in him should not perish but have eternal life. For God did not send his Son into the world to condemn the world, but in order that the world might be saved through him.

JOHN 3:16-17 ESV

ELEVEN
JUDGEMENT

Question:

WHAT SHOULD I KNOW ABOUT GOD'S WRATH?

What does the WORD say:

Calling to the mountains and rocks, "Fall on us and hide us from the face of him who is seated on the throne, and from the wrath of the Lamb, for the great day of their wrath has come, and who can stand?"

REVELATION 6:16-17 ESV

For the mystery of lawlessness is already at work. Only he who now restrains it will do so until he is out of the way. And then the lawless one will be revealed, whom the Lord Jesus will kill with the breath of his mouth and bring to nothing by the appearance of his coming. The coming of the lawless one is by the activity of Satan with all power and false signs and wonders, and with all wicked deception for those who are perishing, because they refused to love the truth and so be saved. Therefore God sends them a strong delusion, so that they may believe what is false, in order that all may be condemned who did not believe the truth but had pleasure in unrighteousness.

2 THESSALONIANS 2:7-12 ESV

Question:

JUDGING OTHERS

What does the WORD say:

Do not judge, or you too will be judged. For in the same way you judge others, you will be judged, and with the measure you use, it will be measured to you. Why do you look at the speck of sawdust in your brother's eye and pay no attention to the plank in your own eye? How can you say to your brother, 'Let me take the speck out of your eye,' when all the time there is a plank in your own eye? You hypocrite, first take the plank out of your own eye, and then you will see clearly to remove the speck from your brother's eye. Do not give dogs what is sacred; do not throw your pearls to pigs. If you do, they may trample them under their feet, and turn and tear you to pieces.

MATTHEW 7: 1-6

Because, if you confess with your mouth that Jesus is Lord and believe in your heart that God raised him from the dead, you will be saved.

ROMANS 10:9 ESV

Question:

WHY IS IT IMPORTANT TO NOT JUDGE?
WHY SHOULD I NOT JUDGE?

What does the WORD say:

You, therefore, have no excuse, you who pass judgment on someone else, for at whatever point you judge another, you are condemning yourself, because you who pass judgment do the same things. 2 Now we know that God's judgment against those who do such things is based on truth. So when you, a mere human being, pass judgment on them and yet do the same things, do you think you will escape God's judgment? Or do you show contempt for the riches of his kindness, forbearance and patience, not realizing that God's kindness is intended to lead you to repentance?

But because of your stubbornness and your unrepentant heart, you are storing up wrath against yourself for the day of God's wrath, when his righteous judgment will be revealed. God "will repay each person according to what they have done." To those who by persistence in doing good seek glory, honor and immortality, he will give eternal life. But for those who are self-seeking and who reject the truth and follow evil, there will be wrath and anger. There will be trouble and distress for every human being who does evil: first for the Jew, then for the Gentile; but glory, honor and peace for everyone who does good: first for the Jew, then for the Gentile. For God does not show favoritism.

ROMANS 2:5-11

TWELVE
LOVE

Question:

WHAT'S THE ONLY THING THAT COUNTS?

What does the WORD say:

For in Christ Jesus neither circumcision nor uncircumcision has any value. The only thing that counts is faith expressing itself through love.

GALATIANS 5:6 NIV

Question:

WHAT IS ABIDING LOVE?

What does the WORD say:

So we have come to know and to believe the love that God has for us. God is love, and whoever abides in love abides in God, and God abides in him.

1 JOHN 4:16 ESV

Question:

WHAT DOES GOD REQUIRE OF ME?

What does the WORD say:

He has told you, O man, what is good; and what does the Lord require of you but to do justice, and to love kindness, and to walk humbly with your God?

MICAH 6:8 ESV

THIRTEEN

PAIN

Question:

WHY DOES PAIN EXIST AND WHY DO WE TOIL
SO MUCH?

What does the WORD say:

To the woman he said, "I will surely multiply your pain in child-bearing; in pain you shall bring forth children. Your desire shall be for your husband, and he shall rule over you." And to Adam he said, "Because you have listened to the voice of your wife and have eaten of the tree of which I commanded you, 'You shall not eat of it,' cursed is the ground because of you; in pain you shall eat of it all the days of your life; thorns and thistles it shall bring forth for you; and you shall eat the plants of the field. By the sweat of your face you shall eat bread, till you return to the ground, for out of it you were taken; for you are dust, and to dust you shall return.

GENESIS 3:16-19

Question:

WHY DOES GOD HEAL SOME AND NOT
OTHERS?

What does the WORD say:

Therefore we must pay much closer attention to what we have
heard, lest we drift away from it. For since the message declared by
angels proved to be reliable, and every transgression or disobedi-
ence received a just retribution, how shall we escape if we neglect
such a great salvation? It was declared at first by the Lord, and it
was attested to us by those who heard, while God also bore witness
by signs and wonders and various miracles and by gifts of the Holy
Spirit distributed according to his will.

HEBREWS 2:1-4 ESV

Question:

WHY DOES GOD LET EVIL HAPPEN?

What does the WORD say:

With whom will you compare me or count me equal? To whom will you liken me that we may be compared? Some pour out gold from their bags and weigh out silver on the scales; they hire a goldsmith to make it into a god, and they bow down and worship it.

They lift it to their shoulders and carry it; they set it up in its place, and there it stands. From that spot it cannot move. Even though someone cries out to it, it cannot answer; it cannot save them from their troubles.

Remember this, keep it in mind, take it to heart, you rebels. Remember the former things, those of long ago; I am God, and there is no other; I am God, and there is none like me.

I make known the end from the beginning, from ancient times, what is still to come. I say, 'My purpose will stand, and I will do all that I please.' From the east I summon a bird of prey; from a far-off land, a man to fulfill my purpose. What I have said, that I will bring about; what I have planned, that I will do.

ISAIAH 40:5-11

Question:

WHY DOES GOD ALLOW BAD THINGS TO
HAPPEN TO GOOD PEOPLE?

What does the WORD say:

Bel bows down; Nebo stoops; their idols are on beasts and live-stock; these things you carry are borne as burdens on weary beasts. They stoop; they bow down together; they cannot save the burden, but themselves go into captivity. "Listen to me, O house of Jacob, all the remnant of the house of Israel, who have been borne by me from before your birth, carried from the womb; even to your old age I am he, and to gray hairs I will carry you. I have made, and I will bear;

I will carry and will save. "To whom will you liken me and make me equal, and compare me, that we may be alike? Those who lavish gold from the purse, and weigh out silver in the scales, hire a goldsmith, and he makes it into a god; then they fall down and worship! They lift it to their shoulders, they carry it, they set it in its place, and it stands there; it cannot move from its place. If one cries to it, it does not answer or save him from his trouble.

"Remember this and stand firm, recall it to mind, you transgressors, remember the former things of old; for I am God, and there is no other; I am God, and there is none like me, declaring the end from the beginning and from ancient times things not yet done, saying, 'My counsel shall stand, and I will accomplish all my purpose,' calling a bird of prey from the east, the man of my counsel from a far country. I have spoken, and I will bring it to pass; I have purposed, and I will do it. "Listen to me, you stubborn of heart, you who are far from righteousness: I bring near my righteousness; it is not far off, and my salvation will not delay; I will put salvation in Zion, for Israel my glory."

ISAIAH 46:1-13 ESV

FOURTEEN
PEACE

Question:

IS JESUS PEACE DIFFERENT FROM WORLD
PEACE?

What does the WORD say:

Peace I leave with you; my peace I give to you. Not as the world gives do I give to you. Let not your hearts be troubled, neither let them be afraid.

JOHN 14:27 ESV

Now faith is the assurance of things hoped for, the conviction of things not seen.

HEBREWS 11:1 ESV

By which he has granted to us his precious and very great promises, so that through them you may become partakers of the divine nature, having escaped from the corruption that is in the world because of sinful desire.

2 PETER 1:4 ESV

Question:

WHAT'S THE SAFEST SHELTER?

What does the WORD say:

He who dwells in the shelter of the Most High will abide in the shadow of the Almighty. I will say to the Lord, "My refuge and my fortress, my God, in whom I trust." For he will deliver you from the snare of the fowler and from the deadly pestilence. He will cover you with his pinions, and under his wings you will find refuge; his faithfulness is a shield and buckler. You will not fear the terror of the night, nor the arrow that flies by day.

PSALM 91:1-16 ESV

Question:

WHAT SHOULD I THINK ABOUT?

What does the WORD say:

Do not be anxious about anything, but in everything by prayer and supplication with thanksgiving let your requests be made known to God. And the peace of God, which surpasses all understanding, will guard your hearts and your minds in Christ Jesus. Finally, brothers, whatever is true, whatever is honorable, whatever is just, whatever is pure, whatever is lovely, whatever is commendable, if there is any excellence, if there is anything worthy of praise, think about these things.

PHILIPPIANS 4:6-8 ESV

FIFTEEN

PRIORITIES

Question:

WHAT ARE YOUR PRIORITIES IN LIFE?

What does the WORD say:

But seek first the kingdom of God and his righteousness, and all these things will be added to you.

MATTHEW 6:33 ESV

In action: Set your alarm every day for 6:33am to remind you to seek first the Kingdom.

Question:

WHAT AM I SUPPOSED TO BE DOING?

What does the WORD say:

I am the vine; you are the branches. If you remain in me and I in you, you will bear much fruit; apart from me you can do nothing.

JOHN 15:5 NIV

So I find this law at work: Although I want to do good, evil is right there with me. For in my inner being I delight in God's law; but I see another law at work in me, waging war against the law of my mind and making me a prisoner of the law of sin at work within me. What a wretched man I am! Who will rescue me from this body that is subject to death? Thanks be to God, who delivers me through Jesus Christ our Lord!

ROMANS 7:21-25 ESV

No longer do I call you servants, for a servant does not understand what his master is doing. But I have called you friends, because everything I have learned from My Father I have made known to you.

JOHN 15:15 ESV

So whoever knows the right thing to do and fails to do it, for him it is sin.

JAMES 4:17 ESV

And let us not grow weary of doing good, for in due season we will reap, if we do not give up.

GALATIANS 6:9 ESV

But be doers of the word and not hearers only, deceiving yourselves.

JAMES 1:22 ESV

Therefore, whether you eat or drink, or whatever you do, do everything for the glory of God.

1 CORINTHIANS 10:31 ESV

And whatsoever you do, in word or deed, do everything in the name of the Lord Jesus, giving thanks to God the Father through him.

COLOSSIANS 3:17 ESV

But seek first his kingdom and his righteousness, and all these things will be given to you as well.

MATTHEW 6:33 NIV

Question:

WHAT MATTERS MOST?

What does the WORD say:

What is more, I consider everything a loss because of the surpassing worth of knowing Christ Jesus my Lord, for whose sake I have lost all things. I consider them garbage, that I may gain Christ and be found in him, not having a righteousness of my own that comes from the law, but that which is through faith in Christ—the righteousness that comes from God on the basis of faith. I want to know Christ—yes, to know the power of his resurrection and participation in his sufferings, becoming like him in his death

PHILIPPIANS 3:8-10 NIV

But that matters little. What matters most to me is to finish what God started: the job the Master Jesus gave me of letting everyone I meet know all about this incredibly extravagant generosity of God. "And so this is good-bye. You're not going to see me again, nor I you, you whom I have gone among for so long proclaiming the news of God's inaugurated kingdom. I've done my best for you, given you my all, held back nothing of God's will for you. "Now it's up to you. Be on your toes - both for yourselves and your congregation of sheep. The Holy Spirit has put you in charge of these people - God's people they are - to guard and protect them. God himself thought they were worth dying for. "I know that as soon as I'm gone, vicious wolves are going to show up and rip into this flock, men from your very own ranks twisting words so as to seduce disciples into following them instead of Jesus. So stay awake and keep up your guard. Remember those three years I kept at it with you, never letting up, pouring my heart out with you, one after another. "Now I'm turning you over to God, our marvelous God whose gracious Word can make you into what he wants you to be and give you everything you could possibly need in this community of holy friends. 33 "I've never, as you so well know, had any taste for wealth or fashion. With these bare hands I took care of my own basic needs and those who worked with me.

ACTS 20:24-34 THE MESSAGE

Question:

WHAT DOES GOD REQUIRE OF ME?

What does the WORD say:

He has told you, O man, what is good; and what does the Lord require of you but to do justice, and to love kindness, and to walk humbly with your God?

MICAH 6:8 ESV

Question:

WHAT'S EXPECTED, REQUIRED, OR ASKED
OF ME?

What does the WORD say:

And now, Israel, what does the Lord your God ask of you but to fear the Lord your God, to walk in obedience to him, to love him, to serve the Lord your God with all your heart and with all your soul, and to observe the Lord's commands and decrees that I am giving you today for your own good?

DEUTERONOMY 10:12-13 NIV

Question:

WHAT MUST WE DO? WHAT DOES GOD WANT
FROM US?

What does the WORD say:

God is spirit, and those who worship him must worship in spirit
and truth.

JOHN 4:24 ESV

Question:

WHAT SHOULD I THINK ABOUT?

What does the WORD say:

Do not be anxious about anything, but in everything by prayer and supplication with thanksgiving let your requests be made known to God. And the peace of God, which surpasses all understanding, will guard your hearts and your minds in Christ Jesus. Finally, brothers, whatever is true, whatever is honorable, whatever is just, whatever is pure, whatever is lovely, whatever is commendable, if there is any excellence, if there is anything worthy of praise, think about these things.

PHILIPPIANS 4:6-8 ESV

Question:

WHAT SHOULD I TREASURE AND COLLECT?

What does the WORD say:

Do not lay up for yourselves treasures on earth, where moth and rust destroy and where thieves break in and steal, but lay up for yourselves treasures in heaven, where neither moth nor rust destroys and where thieves do not break in and steal. For where your treasure is, there your heart will be also.

MATTHEW 6:19-21 ESV

SIXTEEN
SIN

Question:

WHAT'S THE PURPOSE OF THE WICKED?

What does the WORD say:

The Lord has made everything for its purpose, even the wicked for
the day of trouble.

PROVERBS 16:4 ESV

Who gave himself for our sins to deliver us from the present evil
age, according to the will of our God and Father

GALATIANS 1:4 ESV

Question:

What is the definition of sin?

What does the WORD say:

But if you show favoritism, you sin and are convicted by the law as lawbreakers. 10 For whoever keeps the whole law and yet stumbles at just one point is guilty of breaking all of it.

JAMES 2:9 NIV

If anyone, then, knows the good they ought to do and doesn't do it, it is sin for them.

JAMES 4:17 NIV

Now listen, you who say, "Today or tomorrow we will go to this or that city, spend a year there, carry on business and make money." Why, you do not even know what will happen tomorrow. What is your life? You are a mist that appears for a little while and then vanishes. Instead, you ought to say, "If it is the Lord's will, we will live and do this or that." As it is, you boast in your arrogant schemes. All such boasting is evil.

JAMES 4:13-16

See what great love the Father has lavished on us, that we should be called children of God! And that is what we are! The reason the world does not know us is that it did not know him. Dear friends, now we are children of God, and what we will be has not yet been made known. But we know that when Christ appears, we shall be like him, for we shall see him as he is. All who have this hope in him purify themselves, just as he is pure.

1 JOHN 3:4

Everyone who sins breaks the law; in fact, sin is lawlessness. But you know that he appeared so that he might take away our sins. And in him is no sin. No one who lives in him keeps on sinning. No one who continues to sin has either seen him or known him.

1 JOHN 3:4-6 NIV

All wrongdoing is sin, and there is sin that does not lead to death.

1 JOHN 5:17

But whoever has doubts is condemned if they eat, because their eating is not from faith; and everything that does not come from faith is sin.

ROMANS 14:23

SEVENTEEN
STRENGTH

Question:

HOW DO WE RENEW OUR STRENGTH?

What does the WORD say:

But they who wait for the Lord shall renew their strength; they shall mount up with wings like eagles; they shall run and not be weary; they shall walk and not faint.

ISAIAH 40:31 ESV

No, in all these things we are more than conquerors through him who loved us. For I am sure that neither death nor life, nor angels nor rulers, nor things present nor things to come, nor powers, nor height nor depth, nor anything else in all creation, will be able to separate us from the love of God in Christ Jesus our Lord.

ROMANS 8:37-39 ESV

All scripture is breathed out by God and profitable for teaching, for reproof, for correction, and for training in righteousness, that the man of God may be complete, equipped for every good work.

2 TIMOTHY 3:16-17

This is good, and it is pleasing in the sight of God our Savior, who desires all people to be saved and to come to the knowledge of the truth.

1 TIMOTHY 2:3-4

Question:

WHERE DOES MY STRENGTH COME FROM?

What does the WORD say:

God is our refuge and strength, a very present help in trouble.

PSALM 46:1 ESV

Question:

WHO SHALL I FEAR?

What does the WORD say:

The Lord is my light and my salvation; whom shall I fear? The Lord is the stronghold of my life; of whom shall I be afraid?

PSALM 27:1 ESV

Question:

WHAT DO I NEED TO DO TO HAVE MORE
ENERGY?

What does the WORD say:

Have you not known? Have you not heard? The Lord is the ever-lasting God, the Creator of the ends of the earth. He does not faint or grow weary; his understanding is unsearchable. He gives power to the faint, and to him who has no might he increases strength. Even youths shall faint and be weary, and young men shall fall exhausted; but they who wait for the Lord shall renew their strength; they shall mount up with wings like eagles; they shall run and not be weary; they shall walk and not faint.

ISAIAH 40:28-31 ESV

For this I toil, struggling with all his energy that he powerfully works within me.

COLOSSIANS 1:29 ESV

I can do all things through him who strengthens me.

PHILIPPIANS4:13 ESV

May you be strengthened with all power, according to his glorious might, for all endurance and patience with joy.

COLOSSIANS 1:11 ESV

But stay awake at all times, praying that you may have strength to escape all these things that are going to take place, and to stand before the Son of Man.

LUKE 21:36 ESV

Repent therefore, and turn again, that your sins may be blotted out, that times of refreshing may come from the presence of the Lord, and that he may send the Christ appointed for you, Jesus, whom heaven must receive until the time for restoring all the things about which God spoke by the mouth of his holy prophets long ago.

ACTS 3:19-21 ESV

The wind blows where it wishes, and you hear its sound, but you do not know where it comes from or where it goes. So it is with everyone who is born of the Spirit.

JOHN 3:8 ESV

For the Lord will vindicate his people and have compassion on his servants, when he sees that their power is gone and there is none remaining, bond or free.

DEUTERONOMY 32:36 ESV

He who dwells in the shelter of the Most High will abide in the shadow of the Almighty. I will say to the Lord, "My refuge and my fortress, my God, in whom I trust." For he will deliver you from the snare of the fowler and from the deadly pestilence. He will cover you with his pinions, and under his wings you will find refuge; his faithfulness is a shield and buckler. You will not fear the terror of the night, nor the arrow that flies by day

PSALM 91:1-16 ESV

EIGHTEEN
TRUST

Question:

WHY SHOULD I BELIEVE (TRUST) THE BIBLE?

What does the WORD say:

All Scripture is God-breathed and is useful for teaching, rebuking, correcting and training in righteousness, so that the servant of God may be thoroughly equipped for every good work.

2 TIMOTHY 3:16-17 NIV

For prophecy never had its origin in the human will, but prophets, though human, spoke from God as they were carried along by the Holy Spirit.

2 PETER 1:21 NIV

Question:

HOW DO WE HAVE THE RIGHT TO BE
CHILDREN OF GOD?

What does the WORD say:

But to all who did receive him, who believed in his name, he gave
the right to become children of God

JOHN 1:12 ESV

Question:

WHAT'S THE SAFEST SHELTER?

What does the WORD say:

He who dwells in the shelter of the Most High will abide in the shadow of the Almighty. I will say to the Lord, "My refuge and my fortress, my God, in whom I trust." For he will deliver you from the snare of the fowler and from the deadly pestilence. He will cover you with his pinions, and under his wings you will find refuge; his faithfulness is a shield and buckler. You will not fear the terror of the night, nor the arrow that flies by day

PSALM 91:1-16 ESV

Question:

WHAT SHOULD I THINK ABOUT?

What does the WORD say:

Do not be anxious about anything, but in everything by prayer and supplication with thanksgiving let your requests be made known to God. And the peace of God, which surpasses all understanding, will guard your hearts and your minds in Christ Jesus. Finally, brothers, whatever is true, whatever is honorable, whatever is just, whatever is pure, whatever is lovely, whatever is commendable, if there is any excellence, if there is anything worthy of praise, think about these things.

PHILIPPIANS 4:6-8 ESV

Question:

WHO SHALL I FEAR?

What does the WORD say:

Of David. The Lord is my light and my salvation; whom shall I fear? The Lord is the stronghold of my life; of whom shall I be afraid?

PSALM 27:1 ESV

NINETEEN
TRUTH

Question:

WHAT IS TRUTH?

What does the WORD say:

Sanctify them in the truth; your word is truth.

JOHN 17:17 ESV

Jesus said to him, "I am the way, and the truth, and the life. No one comes to the Father except through me.

JOHN 14:6 ESV

Question:

WHAT SHOULD I THINK ABOUT?

What does the WORD say:

Do not be anxious about anything, but in everything by prayer and supplication with thanksgiving let your requests be made known to God. And the peace of God, which surpasses all understanding, will guard your hearts and your minds in Christ Jesus. Finally, brothers, whatever is true, whatever is honorable, whatever is just, whatever is pure, whatever is lovely, whatever is commendable, if there is any excellence, if there is anything worthy of praise, think about these things.

PHILIPPIANS 4:6-8 ESV

TWENTY
WISDOM

Question:

WHAT MUST ONE DO TO BE WISE?

What does the WORD say:

Everyone then who hears these words of mine and does them will be like a wise man who built his house on the rock.

MATTHEW 7:24 ESV

All Scripture is breathed out by God and profitable for teaching, for reproof, for correction, and for training in righteousness.

2 TIMOTHY 3:16 ESV

TWENTY-ONE
WORSHIP

Question:

WHAT MUST WE DO? WHAT DOES GOD WANT
FROM US?

What does the WORD say:

God is spirit, and those who worship him must worship in spirit
and truth.

JOHN 4:24 ESV

Question:

WHAT DOES GOD WANT US TO DELIGHT IN?

What does the WORD say:

Delight yourself in the Lord, and he will give you the desires of your heart.

PSALM 37:4 ESV

Question:

WHAT'S EXALTED ABOVE ALL THINGS?

What does the WORD say:

I bow down toward your holy temple and give thanks to your name for your steadfast love and your faithfulness, for you have exalted above all things your name and your word.

PSALM 138:2 ESV

All Scripture is breathed out by God and profitable for teaching, for reproof, for correction, and for training in righteousness.

2 TIMOTHY 3:16 ESV

Now the Lord is the Spirit, and where the Spirit of the Lord is, there is freedom.

2 CORINTHIANS 3:17 ESV

When Jesus had spoken these words, he lifted up his eyes to heaven, and said, "Father, the hour has come; glorify your Son that the Son may glorify you, since you have given him authority over all flesh, to give eternal life to all whom you have given him. And this is eternal life, that they know you the only true God, and Jesus Christ whom you have sent. I glorified you on earth, having accomplished the work that you gave me to do. And now, Father, glorify me in your own presence with the glory that I had with you before the world existed.

JOHN 17:1-26 ESV

RESOURCES

RECOMMENDED READING

Evidence That Demands a Verdict: Life-Changing Truth for a Skeptical World - Josh McDowell
    https://amzn.to/3DdmiHP

When Skeptics Ask: A Handbook on Christian Evidences - Norman Geisler
    https://amzn.to/3NxrpqW

The Origin of the Bible - Philip Comfort
    https://amzn.to/3PEtFPU

The Case for Christ: A Journalist's Personal Investigation of the Evidence for Jesus - Lee Strobel
    https://amzn.to/443IUGn

Cold-Case Christianity: A Homicide Detective Investigates the Claims of the Gospels - J. Warner Wallace
   https://amzn.to/3CW6HfA

The Purpose-Driven Life: What on Earth Am I Here For? - Rick Warren
   https://amzn.to/3ptIFFA

ONLINE RESOURCES:

Coach Through the Bible - Dennis Blevins
    https://coachtheBible.com/

The Navigators Ministry
    https://www.navigators.org/

Kingdom Living - George La Du
    https://kingdomliving.global

ABOUT THE AUTHOR

John J. Knoernschild grew up in Mount Vernon, WA, with a unique cultural background – a Japanese mother and a German-American father, who proudly served 25 years in the US Navy. He grew up attending church and learned biblical truths from Pastor Warren Schumacher. In high school, he explored Philosophy through Dave Cornelius, engaging with ideas from Aquinas, Pascal, Socrates, and Nietzsche.

After graduating with honors, he pursued further studies at the University of Washington. John returned to Mount Vernon, where he met his wife, Kim at Bible study. Pastor Ron Caulkins encouraged them to move to Portland, Oregon, where John attended Multnomah Bible College under mentors like Dr. Jeff Arthur.

Passionate about spiritual growth, John actively sought spiritual leaders who deepened his faith including Pastor Don Hansen (spiritual warfare), Pastor Larry Henderson (spiritual gifts), and Pastor George La Du (The Identity Project). John's passion for learning and sharing knowledge led him to become a Certified Biblical Entrepreneur Teacher under Patrice Tsague. He co-hosted a Christian radio show called "The Garden Samurai - Wisdom from the Garden of Life" on KKPZ and KPDQ, which is now available as a podcast – a venture that was made possible thanks to the encouragement of his friend, James Autry.

John enjoyed teaching Sunday school with Pastor Dennis Blevins, a life and leadership coach with the Navigators, while being an active member of Anthem Church.

In pursuit of personal growth and expertise, John became certificated as a professional life coach from New Vibe Training. He is also a Brain Health Advocate student studying under Dr. Daniel Amen and Amen University.

John J Knoernschild is a Certified Professional Development Success Coach, dedicated to transforming mindsets and empowering individuals to lead better-quality lives. As the founder of Garden Samurai Coaching and Consulting, he plants the seeds of truth in those he encounters. A talented writer, speaker, and seeker of God's greatness, John currently resides in Oregon City, Oregon, where he continues to make a positive impact on the lives of others.

For more information about John and his work, visit his website: www.gardensamurai.com

Stay connected with John on linktr.ee/johnjknoernschild

ACKNOWLEDGMENTS

To my loving wife, Kim Knoernschild, my best friend for 29 years and counting.

To my two wonderful children, supportive friends, and family, thank you for being my pillars of strength and encouragement throughout this journey.

Special gratitude to my brothers Keith and Hal Knoernschild, whose unwavering support has been a constant source of inspiration.

I am deeply grateful to my parents, Keiko and Joseph Knoernschild, for instilling in me a strong foundation in faith and the Word.

To my in-laws, Mark and Julie Bistranin, thank you for your love and acceptance.

A heartfelt tribute to my spiritual mother, Pam Frisbie (Dandliker).

A special thank you to Julie Pershing, my publisher and friend.

A special thanks to Dennis Blevins, Dr. Thomas Abshier, and to the countless others who have been a part of my life journey.

Brittani Klepich, Donna Darling, Brendin Jobin, Mona Kruger, Veille Arthur, and my BNI Portland Advantage family.

A shout out to my Fire Pit mens group: John E. Flabetich, Tracy Pyett, Matt Yates, Danny Green, Jack Loomis, Rick Sovereign, Sean Denheart, Chip Avery, Adam Albrecht, Mikel Fair, Paul Hoag, and Alex Kettles.

BIC Brothers.: Micheal Bryant, Rico Kaplan, Isham Harris, Reggie Guyton, Robert Christopher, Benny Carson, Mario Denton, Eddie Jordan, Jess McKinley, Brent Parker, Robert Perry, Richard Russell, and Esau Williams.

The IP Group: George La Du, Brad Thomas, Ted Hillison, Dan Terry, Chris Heerdegen, and Boones Bergma.

Mike Lee, James Autry, Tim Moore, Roger Smith, Paul Van Sickle, and my radio ministry brothers.

Kris Rohweder-Lawrence, Ginny (Gabby) Blackburn and my high school friends.

Kellie Grille, Jerry Fletcher, Thomas Clute, and my National Speakers Academy friends.

Pastor Don and Yvonne Hanson (former pastor of NE Baptist Church)

David Fromader, David Chown, and Larry Henderson (former City Bible Church)

Bob Black, Carl Casanova, Carlos Baca, George Vartonof, Joel Day, Roger Shipman, and New Vibe Training

Dave Lien, Dean Taylor, Jim Griffith, Kareen Mills, Bill Stotts, Brian Shimer, Jim Lewis, Elman Brozovsky, Douglas Johnson, Diane Dennis, and Greg Stephens.

Dr. Michael Checkis, Dale Campbell, Luis Palau, and Dr. Joe Aldrich, who have passed to the other side of glory.

To those who inspired me:

- Billy Graham Evangelistic Association
- Luis Palau Evangelistic Association
- Multnomah University
- Gateway Bible Church
- Navigators Ministry
- Anthem Church
- Pedro Adao
- Rick Warren
- Dr. Daniel Amen

And countless others who have influenced my life.

I pray this book brings hope to my children, their spouses, and my nieces, as they discover and embrace the truth of God.

Please help me spread the message that God loves you.

With heartfelt appreciation,

John

It's time to share your story

We're here to help you,
every step of the way.

www.gallivantpress.com

Made in United States
Troutdale, OR
09/27/2023

13233869R00090